Rain Forest Animals

Illustrations by Paul Hess

Text by JoAnn Early Macken

Gareth Stevens Publishing
A WORLD ALMANAC EDUCATION GROUP COMPANY

Please visit our web site at: www.garethstevens.com
For a free color catalog describing Gareth Stevens Publishing's
list of high-quality books and multimedia programs,
call 1-800-542-2595 or fax your request to (414) 332-3567.

For my parents, Lyn and Erich — P. H.
For The Hive, my classmates in the Vermont College MFA in Writing for Children Program — J. E. M.

Library of Congress Cataloging-in-Publication Data

Macken, JoAnn Early.
     Rain forest animals / text by JoAnn Early Macken; illustrations by Paul Hess.
        p. cm. — (Animal worlds)
     Includes bibliographical references.
     Summary: Simple text and illustrations introduce various animals that live in rain forests.
     ISBN 0-8368-3041-5 (lib. bdg.)
     1. Rain forest animals—Juvenile literature. [1. Rain forest animals.] I. Hess, Paul, ill.
II. Title.
QL112.M27   2002
591.734—dc21   2001054162

This North American edition first published in 2002 by
Gareth Stevens Publishing
A World Almanac Education Group Company
330 West Olive Street, Suite 100
Milwaukee, Wisconsin 53212 USA

Book design: Sarah Godwin and Suzy McGrath
Gareth Stevens cover design: Katherine A. Goedheer
Gareth Stevens series editor: Dorothy L. Gibbs

Printed in the United States of America

1 2 3 4 5 6 7 8 9 06 05 04 03 02

Table of Contents

Rain Forests

The weather is warm and wet all year in a rain forest. More types of animals live in rain forests than anywhere else in the world. The animals live at every level. Termites crawl on the damp forest floor. Snakes wind around tree trunks. Birds dart between branches. At the top, they can feel sun and rain.

Monkey

Monkeys swing from branch to branch. They cling to trees and vines with their hands, feet, and tails. They eat almost anything they find.

Parrot

Parrots screech and squawk
in the tops of the trees. Their
brightly colored feathers blend
in with the jungle plants.

Anteater

Anteaters sniff for food with their long snouts. Their sharp claws dig into ant or termite nests. They lick up the insects with their long, sticky tongues.

Snake

Snakes slide on smooth, scaly bodies. Some snakes have patterns or colors that help them hide. A snake sheds its skin to keep growing.

Jaguar

Jaguars are the most active after dark. They hunt on the ground or in water. Black rings circle many of the spots on their fur coats.

Toucan

Toucans live in holes in trees. Their huge bills look heavy, but they are hollow and light. Two toes point forward on each foot, and two point backward.

Tapir

Tapirs crash through the forest at night. They jump into rivers and swamps. They love to swim. They look like pigs, but their snouts are short trunks.

Tree Frog

Tree frogs climb up smooth, wet leaves. Their sticky toes and fingers keep them from sliding off. All night long, they sing.

More Books to Read

Deep in a Rainforest. Gwen Pascoe
   (Gareth Stevens)

First Book about Animals of the Forests.
   (Gareth Stevens)

The Great Kapok Tree: A Tale of the
   Amazon Rain Forest. Lynne Cherry
   (Harcourt Brace)

Red-Eyed Tree Frog. Joy Cowley (Scholastic)